# WHALES

Erik D. Stoops, Jeffrey L. Martin &
Debbie Lynne Stone

Sterling Publishing Co., Inc.
New York

**Library of Congress Cataloging-in-Publication Data**

Stoops, Erik D., 1966–
    Whales / by Erik D. Stoops, Jeffrey L. Martin, and Debbie Lynne Stone.
        p.    cm.
    Includes index.
    ISBN 0-8069-0566-2
    1. Whales—Miscellanea—Juvenile literature.    [1. Whales—
Miscellanea.  2. Questions and answers.]   I. Martin, Jeffrey L.
II. Stone, Debbie Lynne.   III. Title.
QL737.C4S77   1995
599.5—dc20                                                    94-47278
                                                                  CIP
                                                                  AC

Cover Photo: False Killer Whales by Mari A. Smultea,
Courtesy of Pacific Whale Foundation

Design by Judy Morgan

2    4    6    8    10    9    7    5    3    1

First paperback edition published in 1996 by
Sterling Publishing Company, Inc.
387 Park Avenue South, New York, N.Y. 10016
© 1995 by Erik D. Stoops, Jeffrey L. Martin and Debbie Lynne Stone
Distributed in Canada by Sterling Publishing
c/o Canadian Manda Group, One Atlantic Avenue, Suite 105
Toronto, Ontario, Canada M6K 3E7
Distributed in Great Britain and Europe by Cassell PLC
Wellington House, 125 Strand, London WC2R 0BB, England
Distributed in Australia by Capricorn Link (Australia) Pty Ltd.
P.O. Box 6651, Baulkham Hills, Business Centre, NSW 2153, Australia
*Printed and bound in Hong Kong*
*All rights reserved*

Sterling ISBN 0-8069-0566-2 Trade
0-8069-0567-0 Paper

# CONTENTS

# HOW WHALES LIVE

*Whales are among the largest living animals on earth. Like dogs, cats, and people, they are mammals. This means that they are warm-blooded and nurse their young. Even though whales spend all their lives in the water, they have to breathe air, just as people do.*

◄ **Whales, dolphins, and porpoises are all members of the whale family. Most of them, such as this Humpback Whale, help each other hunt for food, watch for enemies and care for their young.**

► **Like other mammals, whales are born live. They don't hatch from eggs. This mother Bowhead Whale keeps close watch over her baby, which is only a few weeks old.**

## How many kinds of whales are there?

There are 13 families of whales, including dolphins and porpoises. Each family has its own distinctive traits. As a group they are all known as cetaceans (si-TA-shunz), or whales. This word comes from the Latin word *cetus*, which means "whale."

## How are whales different from dolphins and porpoises?

Dolphins and porpoises are actually small whales. Dolphins have beak-like faces and are larger than porpoises. Porpoises have round faces and chunkier bodies than dolphins. They are also faster swimmers.

By Mari A. Smultea, courtesy of Pacific Whale Foundation

By D. Rugh

# Do any other mammals live in the water?

Seals, sea lions, and manatees (MAN-uh-teez) also live in the water most of the time. Although they are mammals, they are not related to whales. Seals and sea lions are more closely related to bears, while manatees are related to elephants!

By Dr. Graham Worthy

◄ Manatees live in tropical marshes and streams. Like whales, they never leave the water, even to have their babies. Believe it or not, sailors once thought these animals were mermaids!

► Sea lions and seals spend most of their time swimming in the ocean and catching fish, but they leave the water to mate and have babies.

By Dr. Graham Worthy

# Where do whales live?

Whales live in every ocean of the world—some in icy, polar waters, others in warmer oceans and seas. Some species live near the shore, but many keep far away from it. Others spend some of their lives in freshwater rivers and lakes.

By Mari A. Smultea, courtesy of Pacific Whale Foundation

By Richard A. Rowlett, IUIB

▲ **The Short-Finned Pilot Whale lives in warm ocean waters all over the world.**

◄ **Belugas live in both fresh and salt water. They usually spend part of the year in rivers or bays, but in summer they migrate to icy polar waters.**

# Why do whales migrate?

In the summer they search for food in the Arctic and Antarctic regions. In the winter, they swim into warm tropical waters to bear their young. Most whales travel thousands of miles between the earth's poles and the equator every year.

# Do all whales migrate?

The largest whales do, but many of the smaller ones do not. They stay in one part of the ocean most of the time. Some dolphins travel between shallow and deep water, but they don't make yearly trips between the poles and the equator, as larger whales do.

◄ This baby Humpback Whale was born in the South Pacific, off Hawaii. Its mother has led it back to her summer feeding area in Alaskan waters, where this picture was taken.

# How can you tell where whales come from and where they go?

Humpback Whales can be identified by the markings on their tail. These are different on every whale. Scientists in various parts of the world photograph the whales and then compare the markings to track individual animals.

▲ Whales' tails are called "flukes."

◄ The white markings on the tail of each Humpback Whale are like the whale's fingerprints.

# Are whales smart?

Most scientists agree that whales are quite intelligent, maybe even more so than people! They have large brains, a sign of intelligence. Many are very curious and playful.

▶ **Many whales, like this Grey Whale, swim right up to whale-watching boats. They seem to want to get a closer look at the people.**

By Thomas Jefferson

By Richard A. Rowlett, IUIB

▲ **Dolphins like to ride the wave at the bow (front) of the boat. This is called bow-riding. It's something like surfing. As dolphins leap out of the water, they seem to be watching the people in the boat. Dolphins also bow-ride in front of large whales.**

# How fast can whales swim?

The fastest large whales may swim up to 18.6 miles (30km) per hour. These large speedsters are the Blue Whale, the Fin Whale, and the Sei Whale. The more blubber, or fat, a whale has, the more slowly it swims. All whales are strong swimmers, and even the slowest ones are much faster than people.

▼ **The Dall's Porpoise is the fastest swimmer. It can swim up to 31 miles (50km) per hour. It kicks up the water like a speedboat.**

By S. Mizroch, N.M.F.S., N.M.M.L.

9

## Do whales usually hang out together?

Yes, they almost always are found swimming together. They are usually friendly animals who live together and pull together to survive.

## Do different kinds of whales get along?

Yes, many kinds of whales may be found in the same group. They are sometimes drawn together because they eat the same food or migrate to the same places.

## Do whales sleep?

Whale sleep is a little like cat-napping. While one half of the whale's brain takes its turn sleeping, the other makes sure that the whale gets to the surface to breathe. This also helps the whale to stay alert to predators.

By NOAA: Keith D. Mullin

▲ Melon-Headed Whales live in groups of up to 1,500 animals. These groups, or herds, are some of the largest of any whale.

▼ A group of whales is also called a "pod." Pods of Humpbacks may be made up of as few as three animals during migration, or as many as a dozen where mothers have their babies.

By Thomas Jefferson

## How long do whales live?

Some whales may live as long as 100 years. It's difficult to say how long many species live, since they may sink or be eaten by other animals when they die.

## Do whales ever get sick?

Yes, dental disease, broken bones, and tumors are a few of the conditions whales live with. Man-made chemicals, such as pesticides, end up in the bodies of whales and make them sick.

By Dr. Bernd Würsig

▲ Small parasites called "whale lice" live in the folds of skin around the whale's eyes, mouth, and throat.

## What is a barnacle?

Barnacles are hard-shelled creatures that attach themselves to underwater objects and animals, such as whales.

## What do whales die of?

They drown in drift nets. Sometimes they are rammed by large ships or killed for food. Whales also die from pesticides and pollution.

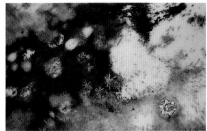

By Mari A. Smultea, courtesy of Pacific Whale Foundation

▲ Whale lice and barnacles have attached themselves to the skin of this Grey Whale.

By NOAA: Wayne Hoggard

▲ The Fin Whale is one of the oldest living whales. It can live to be 100 years old.

# What is "breaching"?

It is called breaching when whales, such as the Humpback, leap straight up into the air. This may be the whale's way of saying, "Hi, everybody," so other whales know it's around. Sometimes, when one whale breaches, others will also. A whale may breach to show off its strength. Sometimes whales jump or breach to confuse fish that they are chasing, or to herd them together. By jumping, they can also travel faster and see farther. Some whales may jump out of the water in order to loosen small animals that are clinging to their skin. Some whales jump so dramatically that they seem to be doing it just for fun!

▶ **Dusky Dolphins like to chase each other. Once one starts jumping, it gets others started. Before you know it, hundreds of Duskies are creating waves in the sea!**

◀ **The Dusky Dolphin is well known for its amazing flips as it leaps out of the water. Duskies may make up to 50 leaps in a row.**

By Dr. Bernd Würsig

By Dr. Bernd Würsig

## What is "sounding"?

Sounding is another word for diving. When a whale is preparing to dive, it usually takes a number of shallow breaths and then one deep breath—and down it goes!

▶ **This Humpback Whale is sounding. Its flukes (tail fins) are high in the air and its body is at a steep angle under the water.**

By Mari A. Smultea, courtesy of Pacific Whale Foundation

## What is "spy hopping"?

Every once in a while whales stick their head above the surface to look around, maybe for other whales or for predators or food. This look-around is called spy hopping.

▶ **This Killer Whale is spy-hopping—holding its head high out of the water.**

By Mari A. Smultea, courtesy of Pacific Whale Foundation

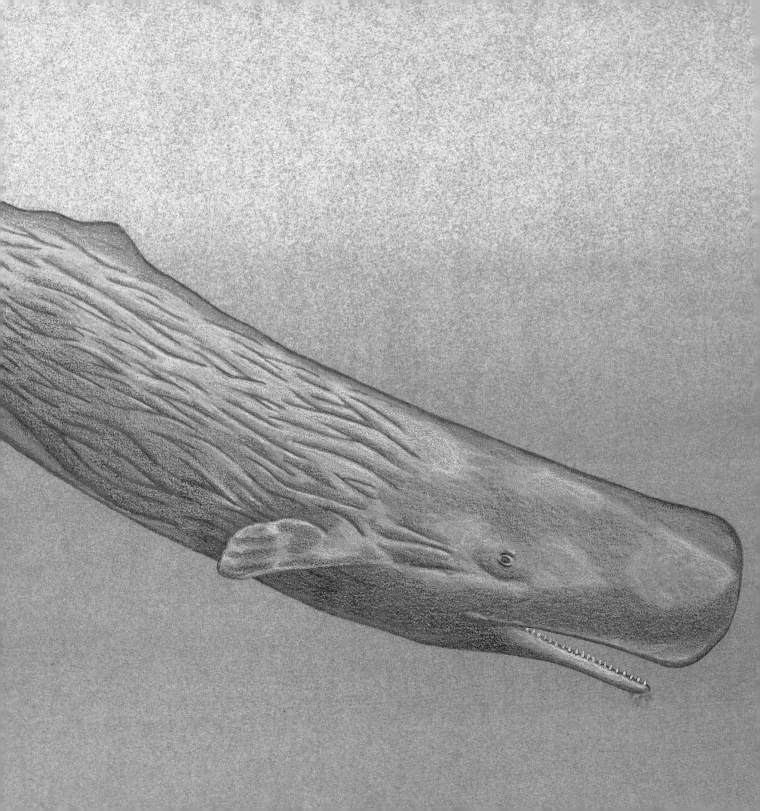

# THE WHALE'S BODY

Whales are very different from land mammals. Instead of legs, they have fins, which are perfect for swimming. Their skin looks shiny, like an inner tube. They have a blowhole for breathing, small eyes, a large mouth, and a gigantic tail. Some are beautifully colored, such as Killer Whales, while others, such as the Grey Whale, are dull-looking.

▶ Belugas are grey when they are born, but get lighter in color as they grow. Adult Belugas are pure white.

◀ The Sperm Whale is famous for its enormous square head.

By Jeffrey L. Martin

## What colors are whales?

The most common whale colors are black, white, light grey, dark grey, and blue-grey. All whales have one or more of these colors on their bodies. A few species also have yellow, tan, and even pink. Some whales have spots or stripes.

Official U.S. Navy Photograph

By NOAA: Carol Roden

▲ The Orca is a beautiful animal, boldly marked in black and white. It is the only whale with a white patch over its eyes.

# Is a whale a fish?

No, the whale looks like a big fish, but it is a marine mammal. It has a blowhole to breathe through, while the shark has gills and gets oxygen directly from the water. The two animals also swim differently.

# What's the difference in the way whales and fish swim?

Whales have a horizontal tail fin. They move it up and down to swim forward in the water. The upward stroke is called the power stroke and the downward stroke is called the recovery stroke. Fish have vertical tails that they move from side to side.

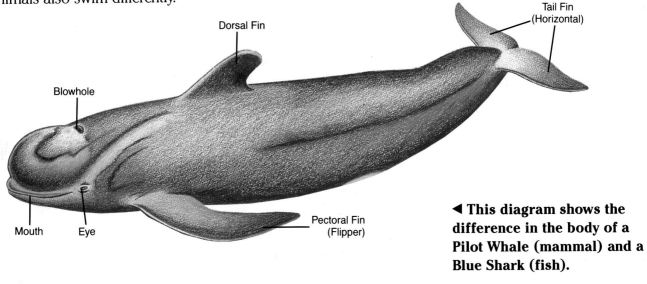

Dorsal Fin

Blowhole

Tail Fin (Horizontal)

Mouth Eye

Pectoral Fin (Flipper)

◀ **This diagram shows the difference in the body of a Pilot Whale (mammal) and a Blue Shark (fish).**

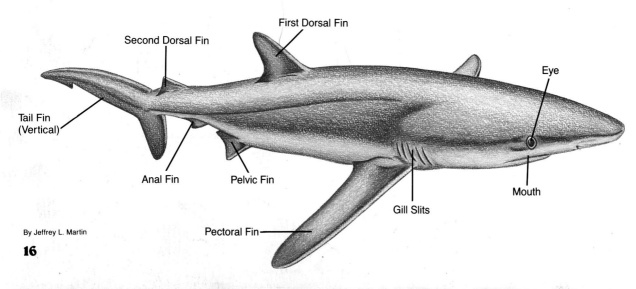

First Dorsal Fin

Second Dorsal Fin

Eye

Tail Fin (Vertical)

Anal Fin Pelvic Fin

Gill Slits

Mouth

Pectoral Fin

By Jeffrey L. Martin

16

# What does a whale's skin feel like?

A whale's skin feels soft and very smooth, like touching a wet inner tube or a vinyl pool raft. Its sleek skin helps it slip easily through the water. Unlike humans, whales have no hair, but some species have whiskers around their mouth.

By Kathleen Dudzinski

By Richard A. Rowlett, IUIB

**◄ Each bump on the head of this Humpback Whale has a whisker-like hair. The whiskers are only half an inch (1.25cm) long and difficult to see.**

# Is it true that whales shed their skin?

Yes, all whales do. The Beluga or White Whale, for example, sheds when it migrates towards the North Pole. It rubs against rocks to get rid of its old, yellowed skin, which comes off in large sheets. Its new skin is white.

**▼ You can see the callosities—the white bumps—on the head of this Right Whale. As the whale gets older, the callosities get bigger.**

# What are "callosities"?

Callosities (kuh-LAHS-uh-teez) are white patches of hardened skin that grow on the heads of Right Whales. They are shaped a little differently on each whale.

# Does a whale have the same kind of bones as people?

A whale's skeleton is not hard like a human's. Its bones are flexible, spongy, and very light. They are filled with fat and oil to help the whale float like a boat. While its bones may be light, the whale's skeleton is huge, so it still weighs a great deal.

▲ A whale's body is supported by water, not by its skeleton. This is one reason why whales are able to grow so large. This skeleton belonged to a female Fin Whale. It's 55 feet (16.7m) long.

▲ A beached whale can suffocate under its own weight, because its ribs are not hard and strong enough to keep its lungs from caving in.

▲ The whale's backbone is actually made up of smaller bones called vertebrae (VERT-a-bray). Long, flat spines on the top and sides of the vertebrae attach to powerful swimming muscles.

▲ The vertebrae in the neck of most species are joined together—fused—so that most whales cannot turn their heads.

# What does a whale's skull look like?

You can't tell the shape of a whale's head simply by looking at its skull. The bones that make up the skull have been pushed back to make room for the organs in the whale's head. Some of these bones overlap. Scientists call this "telescoping."

By Richard A. Rowlett, IUIB

◀ **This is the skull of a Sperm Whale. You can see teeth in the lower jaw.**

▼ **Here is what a whale looks like inside. This is a Fin Whale.**

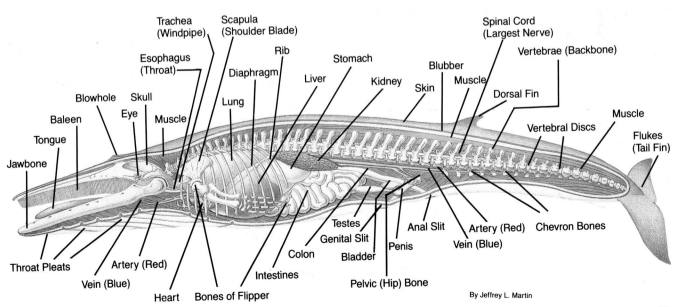

Trachea (Windpipe)
Scapula (Shoulder Blade)
Rib
Stomach
Spinal Cord (Largest Nerve)
Vertebrae (Backbone)
Esophagus (Throat)
Diaphragm
Liver
Kidney
Blubber
Muscle
Dorsal Fin
Blowhole
Skull
Lung
Skin
Muscle
Vertebral Discs
Muscle
Baleen
Eye
Muscle
Flukes (Tail Fin)
Tongue
Jawbone
Testes
Anal Slit
Artery (Red)
Chevron Bones
Genital Slit
Penis
Vein (Blue)
Throat Pleats
Colon
Bladder
Artery (Red)
Vein (Blue)
Intestines
Pelvic (Hip) Bone
Heart
Bones of Flipper

By Jeffrey L. Martin

19

## How many fins do whales have?

Many whales have five fins: a pair just behind the head, called "flippers"; a pair of tail fins that push them through the water; and usually also a fin on their back, called the "dorsal" fin. They are flattened to cut easily through the water.

## What does the whale do with its flippers?

Flippers help the whale steer its way through the water. The flippers have joints that are located in about the same place as our elbows, but the whale can't bend its flippers. They became stiff as the whale evolved. Now the whale rolls its flippers at the shoulder to help it steer.

By Mari A. Smultea, courtesy of Pacific Whale Foundation

◀ This Humpback is slapping the water with its flippers.

▼ A whale's flippers have the same kind of bones that land mammals have in their front legs. This is how scientists know the whale's ancestors lived on land.

By Mari A. Smultea, courtesy of Pacific Whale Foundation

# What are the tail fins like?

The tail fins (flukes) look like two wings at the end of the whale's tail. Unlike the flippers, the flukes did not evolve from legs. They have no bones in them. They are supported by tough, fiber-like tissues known as ligaments. Ligaments are like rubber bands that stretch and make movement easier. We have ligaments in our knees, elbows, hips, and shoulders.

# What is the dorsal fin used for?

The dorsal fin, on the whale's back, helps to keep the whale from rolling from side to side when it swims. An airplane rudder works the same way. Without a rudder, it would be difficult to keep the airplane flying straight.

▶ **The dorsal fin sits high on the back of some whales. Like the flukes, the dorsal fin has no bones in it.**

By Mari A. Smultea, courtesy of Pacific Whale Foundation

▲ **The flukes of this Humpback Whale, like those of all whales, are horizontal—parallel to the water.**

▼ **The Blue Whale's flukes can measure over 15 feet (4.5m) across. You could park a pickup truck on them and still have room left over.**

By Thomas Jefferson

By Mari A. Smultea, courtesy of Pacific Whale Foundation

**21**

# Do whales get cold?

Water absorbs heat 25 times faster than air, so even in warm tropical water a whale can lose body heat. Since many whales spend at least part of their lives in icy water, they have to find ways to stay warm.

# How do whales keep warm in icy water?

A thick layer of fat—known as blubber—lies just beneath their skin. It acts like a layer of clothing, covering the whale's whole body and keeping it warm even in the coldest waters.

▶ **This Bowhead Whale has a layer of blubber that is nearly 20 inches (50cm) thick— thicker than that of any other whale.**

# How do whales keep warm?

Whales are warm-blooded, which means they have the ability to control their body heat. The whale's body temperature is about 98° F (37° C), which is very close to a human's. All mammals and birds are warm-blooded. They generate heat by converting food into energy. Cold-blooded animals, such as crocodiles, need the sun's heat to keep warm.

▶ **A whale's large size also keeps it from losing too much heat. Small animals lose body heat much faster than large animals, like these Southern Right Whales.**

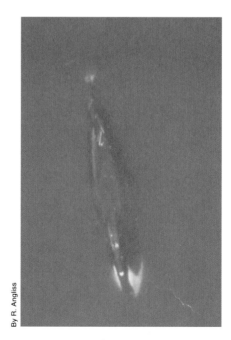

By R. Angliss

By Dr. Bernd Würsig

By Dr. Bernd Würsig

▲ **Whales do not need to take a breath very often. This means that they don't lose as much heat from breathing as people do. When you see your breath on a cold day, that's a sign that heat is escaping.**

# Can whales get too warm?

Yes, a whale can actually overheat if it swims fast for a long period of time. This can be dangerous, causing a whale to become exhausted and drown. But the whale has special ways to cool off.

▶ **Whales, like this Bryde's Whale, can control their blood flow to help cool themselves down.**

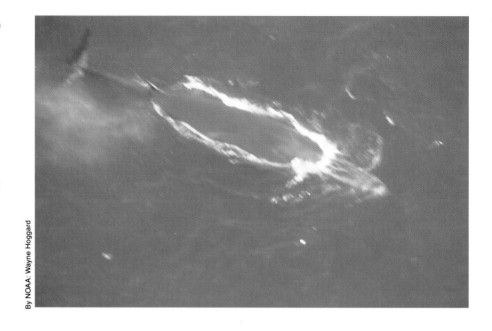

By NOAA: Wayne Hoggard

By Mari A. Smultea, courtesy of Pacific Whale Foundation

▲ **This Humpback Whale shows another way to cool off, which is to stop and rest.**

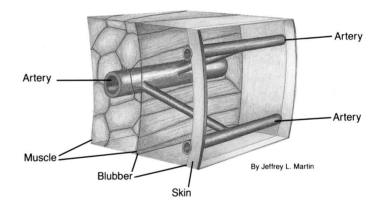

Artery

Artery

Artery

Muscle

Blubber

Skin

By Jeffrey L. Martin

▲ Whales have large blood vessels that carry blood to the skin and fins. To prevent overheating, more blood flows to the skin. The water absorbs the heat from the whale's skin, cooling the whale down, the way a car's radiator cools the engine.

# How do whales breathe?

Whales have lungs and breathe air just like you do. They have to hold their breath when they swim or dive under water.

By Michael W. Newcomer

◀ Instead of having nostrils at the tip of its nose, a whale has them high on the top of its head. Its nostrils are called the "blowhole."

By Richard A. Rowlett, IUIB

▲ Like all whales that don't have teeth, this Humpback Whale has a double blowhole on the top of its head.

By Kathleen Dudzinski

By Richard A. Rowlett, IUIB

◀ Whales, like this Minke Whale, are able to fill and empty their lungs more completely in one breath than most other animals. Nearly all the air in each breath the whale takes in is new. Only about one sixth of the air humans take in is new.

▲ The blowhole is the first part to break the water's surface when the whale comes up to breathe. Because of this, a whale does not have to stop or slow down to breathe.

# How long can a whale hold its breath?

Normally, whales hold their breath for a minute or less. Some whales, though, can stay underwater for 45 minutes or more while looking for food.

By Dagmar C. Fertl

▶ The blowhole of the Sperm Whale is near the front of its head and a little to the left, but the blowholes of most other whales are set farther back.

By Richard A. Rowlett, IUIB

▶ Basilosaurus (buh-SIL-uh-sor-us), one of the earliest whales, first appeared over 50 million years ago, and was 70 feet (21m) long. If you look closely, you'll see its blowhole is halfway between its nose and the top of its forehead.

By Jeffrey L. Martin, courtesy of the Smithsonian Institution

▲ These Southern Right Whale Dolphins are breathing out underwater. You can see their bubble trails on their backs. They will come to the surface before breathing in.

▶ A whale's skin is very sensitive around the blowhole. It can feel the differences in the temperature and pressure of air and water.

By Thomas Jefferson

25

## How do these whales hold their breath for so long?

Whales, like all animals, need oxygen to survive, but they have some special abilities that other animals do not. They store oxygen in their blood, muscles, and smaller blood vessels, and are able to send oxygen-rich blood to the most important parts of the body: the brain and the heart. They can also slow down their heart so that it takes longer to use up their oxygen supply.

## What is spermaceti?

Spermaceti is an oil that is found in huge amounts in the head of the Sperm Whale. The deeper the whale dives, the thicker and waxier the spermaceti gets. It gives the Sperm Whale its name.

By Richard A. Rowlett, IUIB

◀ **The Sperm Whale is a champion diver! Some scientists believe it can dive down from 6,600 to 10,000 feet (2,000 to 3,050m), and stay underwater for more than an hour.**

# How does a whale keep from drowning?

Powerful muscles keep the blowhole shut tight when the whale swims or dives under-water. When the blowhole is closed, the whale's muscles are actually at rest. The whale must want to take a breath to open its blowhole.

By Kathleen Dudzinski

By Thomas Jefferson

▲ This Humpback Whale has just come to the water's surface to breathe. As it breathes out, a vapor cloud called the "spout" or "blow" shoots up in the air.

◄ The Blue Whale can spout a column of water that is over 30 feet (9m) high. That's as high as a three-storey house.

## What is the spout made of?

The spout, or blow, is made up of tiny droplets of water and oil from the lungs of the whale, along with the old air. The spout, or blow, looks different in each whale species.

# THE WHALE'S SENSES

*Living in water is a lot different from living on land. Sound travels farther in water, but light travels farther in air. The whale's senses have evolved to meet the needs of living in the water.*

◀ **This Killer Whale, like other whales, has excellent eyesight. But even when water is at its clearest, it can only see up to about 100 feet (30m) away.**

## Do whales see clearly?

Yes, whales see clearly in both water and air, while humans just see clearly in the air. That's why you need a diving mask to see well underwater, because you need air to see through.

## How do a whale's eyes work?

A whale's eyes are tiny, compared to its body. The eyes of even the largest whales are no bigger than a tennis ball. Because the whale's eyes are on the sides of its head, the whale can see off to the side or a little to the back, but it can't see anything right in front of it.

## Can whales see in the dark?

Yes, the whale's vision has often been compared to the cat's. Many whales hunt in total darkness. Some species feed only at night.

▼ **Sperm Whales often feed in waters that are too deep for light to reach.**

## Do whales have eyelids?

Yes, and they can close their eyes, just as humans can.

▼ **A whale's eye has a strong lens to focus light. A whale can also adjust the size of its pupil (the black part of the eye) to deal with dim and bright light. This is the eye of a Minke Whale.**

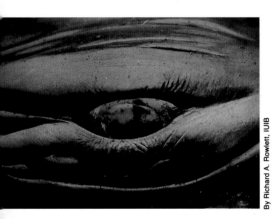

By Richard A. Rowlett, IUIB

## Do whales cry?

No, they don't have tear glands to clean their eyes as people do. Throughout their lives, they secrete thin, transparent mucous from their eyes that make it look as if they're crying, but they're not.

## What color are a whale's eyes?

The Minke Whale has grey eyes, while the eyes of other species range from grey to brown.

## Do whales have ears?

Though the whale has only a tiny earhole, it has an inner ear and can hear very well. Many scientists think that the earhole is useless. In many whales, it is plugged by layers of skin and ear wax.

▼ **If you look closely, you can see the earhole just a few inches behind the eye of this Beluga.**

By Richard A. Rowlett, IUIB

# What can whales hear?

Whales can hear all the sounds that we hear, plus sounds that are too high- and too low-pitched for us. They can hear other whales, fishes, and boats. Whales also hear echoes of sounds they make. They learn about their surroundings by using these echoes. Scientists call this "echolocation" (ekko-lo-KA-shun).

**▼ This diagram shows how whales echolocate.**

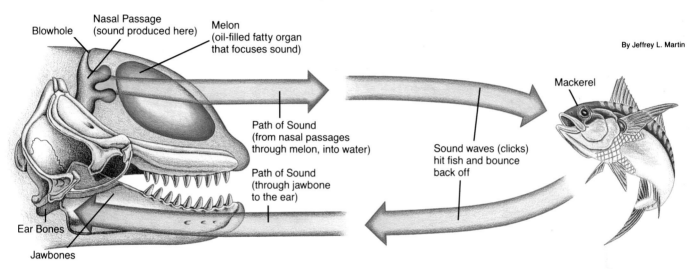

Blowhole

Nasal Passage (sound produced here)

Melon (oil-filled fatty organ that focuses sound)

By Jeffrey L. Martin

Path of Sound (from nasal passages through melon, into water)

Path of Sound (through jawbone to the ear)

Sound waves (clicks) hit fish and bounce back off

Mackerel

Ear Bones

Jawbones

# How do whales use echoes?

The whale makes clicking sounds to locate objects, prey, or other whales. When a whale clicks, the sound travels through the water to the object and bounces off, like a ball bouncing off a wall. If the sound comes back to the whale quickly, the animal knows the object is close by. If the sound comes back slowly, the whale knows the object is far away. It can tell the size, shape, and location of this object, as well as how fast it is going.

**▶ Not all whales echolocate. Whales that have teeth, such as these Pilot Whales, echolocate. Most whales that don't have teeth do not.**

By Mari A. Smultea, courtesy of Pacific Whale Foundation

31

## What is the bump on the forehead of many whales?

It is a fatty organ called the "melon." Scientists believe whales focus the sounds they make through the melon, like light through a lens.

By NOAA: Keith D. Mullin

## How far away does echolocation work?

Whales can echolocate objects up to 2,500 feet (800m) away.

▲ The hearing of a toothed whale, such as this Spinner Dolphin, is sensitive enough to tell whether or not a fish is one that it likes to eat, even from far away.

► A whale, such as this Blainsville Beaked Whale, uses echolocation to find its way around. As sounds bounce off the ocean floor, it memorizes the patterns. Soon it knows the area as well as you know your own room.

By Jon Stern

## Do whales keep coming back to the same part of the ocean?

Usually they do. Even whales that migrate go to and from the same feeding and calving grounds.

▼ **Sometimes shallow water confuses the whale and its echolocation doesn't work properly. That may be why this Risso's Dolphin stranded itself and died.**

By Richard A. Rowlett IUIB

By Thomas Jefferson

▲ **Most toothed whales, like this Beluga, have a melon, but "baleen whales"—those without teeth—don't. This is because baleen whales don't echolocate.**

33

## What is "stranding"?

When one or more whales swim ashore and beach themselves—or are unable to get back into the water—it is called a stranding.

## Why do whales get stranded?

There may be many reasons, including pollution or natural causes such as old age. But scientists aren't sure why sometimes whole herds of healthy whales will strand themselves. It may be because they become confused by shallow waters and sloping ocean floors. Sometimes, if one member of a pod becomes stranded, the rest will follow.

By Dr. Graham Worthy

▲ Sick or dying whales often enter shallow water to rest. This Grey Whale was weakened after it became tangled in a fishing net. Since Grey Whales sink when they die, it's a safe guess that it became stranded while it was still alive.

## What other sounds do whales make?

Whales "talk" in whistles, chirps, grunts, and groans. Humpback Whales, for example, are famous for their "singing," an eerie collection of bellowing, creaking, moaning, and whistling. Only the males sing, and each has his own song that lasts 20 minutes or so. Then he sings the same song again. Each year, the Humpback's song sounds a little different from the year before. Scientists can identify individual Humpbacks by their song.

## How do whales make sounds?

Whales make sounds by squeezing air through their windpipes and blowholes. They have no vocal cords, so they can't make sounds the way humans do.

▶ **Dolphin and porpoise language is a little different from that of larger whales. It sounds to us like clicks, squeaks, pops and whistles.**

By Kathleen Dudzinski

▲ **Humpback Whales call to each other from distances of thousands of miles. Other** whales call to each other, too, but Humpbacks are the best "singers."

By Thomas Jefferson.

By Kathleen Dudzinski

## What do whales feel?

Whales have very sensitive skin, especially around the blowhole, where they do not like to be touched. They can feel heat and cold, and can sense tiny changes in pressure around their bodies.

▲ Whales touch their companions with their flukes, flippers or mouths. They also rub their bodies against other whales, as these dolphins are doing, sometimes just in play.

36

## Can whales smell things?

Since whales hold their breath most of the time, it is possible that their nostrils may no longer have the nerves that sense smells.

## Do whales taste their food?

We don't really know whether the majority of whales have a sense of taste. Imagine doing taste tests with 60-foot wild creatures while being tossed around in the open ocean! The only experiments have been with small, captive whales, such as Bottlenose Dolphins. It seems that they do have a sense of taste. They can tell if a fish is fresh, and they will not eat rotten fish.

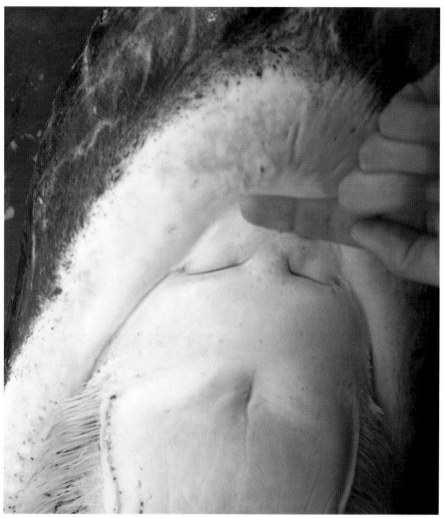

By Jon Stern

▲ The slits at the tip of the upper lip of this Grey Whale are the openings to the Jacobsen's Organ. Scientists don't know for sure the purpose of this organ in whales, but in animals such as snakes the organ helps sense smells.

# EATING HABITS

*We have already seen that some whales have teeth and some don't. They have very different eating habits. "Toothed whales," such as the Sperm Whale, actively hunt their food. "Baleen (buh-LEEN) whales," such as the Blue Whale, cruise through the water like giant vacuum cleaners, scooping up the tiniest creatures in the sea.*

◄ **All whales eat other animals. Some whales may even attack other whales for dinner. These Humpback Whales are lunge-feeding (see page 42).**

(see page 42)

By Thomas Jefferson

## How do baleen whales get their food?

Instead of teeth, baleen whales have bristly strands called "baleen" filling their mouths. They feed by scooping up thousands of gallons of water in their mouths as they swim.

▼ **The baleen hangs down from the roof of the whale's mouth. It is made of keratin (KER-uh-tin), the same material as your fingernails. This is the baleen of a Minke Whale.**

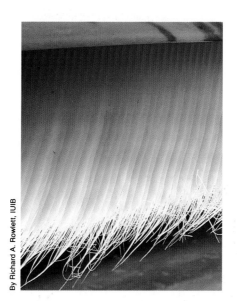

By Richard A. Rowlett, IUIB

Their huge tongue squeezes out the water, and their food is trapped in the fringes of the baleen. Then all they have to do is swallow. This is called filter-feeding.

By National Marine Mammal Laboratory

▲ **Another word for baleen whales is "mysticetes" (MISS-ti-SEE-teez), which means "moustache whale" in Greek. Baleen whales, like this Grey Whale, look as if they have moustaches.**

## What do baleen whales eat?

Most baleen whales eat plankton, tiny animals that drift with the currents. Plankton live near the ocean's surface and cannot travel far on their own.

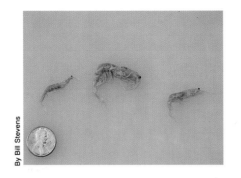

By Bill Stevens

◄ **One type of plankton is krill, tiny shrimp that swarm by the millions in the upper layers of the ocean. The Blue Whale may eat from one to four tons of krill a day.**

## Are there many kinds of baleen whale?

There are 11 types, and they are the largest whales. Only two of them are under 45 feet (14m) long.

▼ **You can see the baleen hanging from the roof of the mouth of this Minke Whale. The baleen of the Bowhead Whale is longer, measuring around 14 feet (4.2 m).**

By D. Rugh

By Richard A. Rowlett, IUIB

▲ **The Bowhead Whale has a huge mouth that measures one third of its body length. Its close relative, the Right Whale, does too.**

By Richard A. Rowlett, IUIB

By Mari A. Smultea, courtesy of Pacific Whale Foundation

▲ This Humpback's throat pleats are expanded. This allows the whale to take in a huge amount of water. More water means more food.

▲ The Minke Whale is one of six species of baleen whale that have pleats (PLEE-ts) on their throat. These pleats can stretch to greatly increase the size of the whale's throat.

▶ The Grey Whale stirs up sand from the ocean bottom, straining out crabs and fish living there. The Grey Whale is the only one that feeds by plowing through the ocean bottom.

By H. Braham

## What is "lunge feeding"?

In lunge feeding, the Humpback Whale corrals a school of fish into a small space. Then it charges up from beneath them, so that they spill into its open mouth.

## Do whales hunt in groups?

Yes, some species, like the Killer Whale, hunt in packs of as many as 30 animals. They surround their prey, such as another whale, and take turns swimming in to attack. They will bite and tear away chunks of flesh and swallow them whole. Other species also feed in smaller groups. Different species of whale may also feed together, because they eat the same foods.

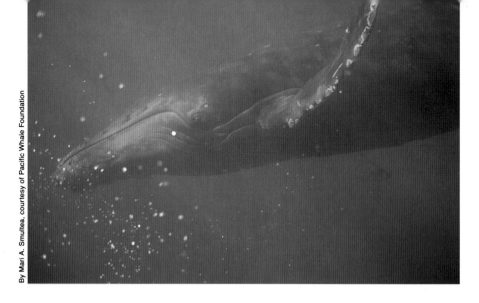

By Mari A. Smultea, courtesy of Pacific Whale Foundation

▲ These Humpbacks are corralling fish—blowing streams of bubbles as they swim in circles around them—and creating a "bubble" net.

## How are toothed whales different from baleen whales?

Toothed whales are faster swimmers. They have to be, so that they can chase the fast-moving animals that they like to eat. They have teeth instead of baleen so that they can catch their prey. Toothed whales also usually dive deeper than baleen whales and stay underwater longer.

## Are toothed whales bigger than baleen whales?

No, most toothed whales are smaller, but they have bigger brains compared to their body size. There are about 66 species of toothed whales, including dolphins and porpoises. Scientists call the family of toothed whales *odontocetes* (oh-DON-toh-SEE-teez), which means "toothed whales" in Latin.

## What do toothed whales eat?

The favorite foods of toothed whales include mackerel, herring and squid—all fast swimmers.

## How do toothed whales catch their food?

Whales catch their food in a variety of ways. Orcas tip ice floes (large drifting chunks of ice) and grab penguins and seals that slip from the ice. Sperm Whales dive down as deep as two miles (3,200m) in search of fish, squid, and octopus.

By Richard A. Rowlett, IUIB

By Richard A. Rowlett, IUIB

▲ This Orca is swimming along an ice edge, searching for penguins and seals. Orcas are called Killer Whales. They are the largest mammal-eaters in the world.

◀ The Sperm Whale is the largest toothed whale. It can grow to a length of 60 feet (18m) and weigh as much as 44 tons (39,600kg).

# Do whales chew their food?

No, whales' teeth are not made for chewing. They only eat food that is small enough to swallow whole. Orcas, which sometimes hunt large whales, rip out bite-size chunks of flesh and swallow the chunks whole. But they do not chew their food.

## How many teeth do whales have?

That depends on the species. Some whales have very few teeth or none at all. Most dolphins have between 100 and 160 teeth. Most porpoises have about 100 teeth. The rest have fewer teeth than this.

▼ **Spinner Dolphins have 250 or more teeth. That's the most teeth of any whale.**

By NOAA: Keith D. Mullin

## What do a whale's teeth look like?

Most whales have pointed, cone-shaped teeth. Some species have sharp, curved teeth. Porpoises' teeth are shaped like little shovels.

By Dagmar C. Fertl

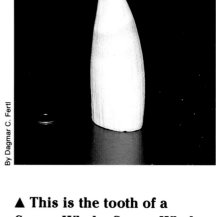

By Dagmar C. Fertl

▲ **This is the tooth of a Sperm Whale. Sperm Whales have 36 to 50 teeth in their lower jaw. Each tooth measures three to eight inches (7.6 to 20.3cm).**

◄ **This man is holding the left jawbone of a Beaked Whale. No species of Beaked Whale has more than two teeth in each side of its jaw. Some have none at all. It's a mystery to scientists how these whales catch fish and squid with so few teeth.**

By Dagmar C. Fertl

## Do whales get two sets of teeth as people do?

Unlike humans, whales get only one set of teeth. If a tooth is lost or worn down, a new tooth does not grow in to replace it.

## How much food do whales eat?

Whales have to eat a lot of food. They need food energy to keep warm and to swim. They don't need to eat all the time, though, since they store energy in their body fat. When there is plenty to eat, the layer of blubber on whales' bodies gets thicker, and the whales "fatten up." When food is scarce, whales live off this layer of fat and it gets thinner.

By Dr. Raymond J. Tarpley, College of Veterinary Medicine, Texas A&M University

▲ The teeth of this older Bottlenose Dolphin are worn down from constant use.

## How long can whales go without eating?

Whales can go several months without food. They don't usually eat during the mating season.

## Do whales drink water?

Whales don't need to drink water, but they may swallow some as they feed. They get their water from the fish they eat and from the blubber in their bodies.

# WHALE REPRODUCTION

*Whales are different from most mammals since they mate and have their babies in the water. Baby whales are called calves. A whale has only one calf every few years.*

◀ **Humpback Whales travel far from their summer feeding grounds in icy, polar waters to warmer waters in the winter to breed.**

▶ **Whales are rarely seen mating or giving birth in the wild. Scientists are still trying to find out more about their reproductive habits.**

## How are male and female whales different?

Among baleen whales, females are much larger than the males. Among toothed whales, males are larger than females. In all species, every whale's belly has a navel and a genital slit. The male's sex organs are tucked inside the genital slit. Females have two additional slits on each side, which are mammary glands that produce milk.

# How do whales court?

In all species, males compete for the right to mate with a female. Many make impressive displays of leaping high out of the water. In most species, females and males touch and chase each other during courtship. Humpback males often sing to attract females. A group of Humpback males from the same area sing the same song. Humpbacks change these songs from year to year, and they always sound different from whales from another area.

▼ **Humpbacks also slap their tails or flippers in a splashy display to get the female's attention.**

By Kathleen Dudzinski

48

## Do whales have only one mate?

Scientists think that all whales have more than one mate, but they're not entirely sure.

## How do whales mate?

When whales mate, they lie belly to belly in the water. Then, the male inserts his reproductive organ into the female's genital slit.

## Where do whales mate?

Some species, such as the Sperm Whale, have special areas where generations of whales have come to mate. Female whales stay together in what is called a "nursery school." Males need to find a nursery school in order to mate.

By Dr. Bernd Würsig

▲ **Male Southern Right Whales, like other species, fight for the right to mate with a female. The winning male mates with the female, as seen here in a breeding area near Patagonia, Argentina.**

## How long does it take a mother to have a baby?

The length of time a whale is pregnant is called the "gestation period." This ranges from 8 to 17 months, depending on the species.

▶ **Humpback Whales give birth after a gestation period of 12 months.**

By Thomas Jefferson

By Jon Stern

◀ **Some toothed whales, such as this Baird's Beaked Whale, have a gestation period that lasts as long as 17 months. Baleen whales generally have shorter pregnancies.**

# Do all whales give live birth?

Yes, like most mammals, all species of whales give live birth to their offspring. Whales are usually born tail first. After the baby comes out, the cord breaks, and the calf is free of its mother.

▼ A Fin Whale calf is being born. Although it is small compared to its mother, the newborn calf is over 20 feet (6.5m) long!

By Jeffrey L. Martin

▶ As soon as the calf is free from its mother, it swims to the surface to take its first breath. The mother will help it to the surface, if necessary. This calf is a Humpback Whale.

By Mari A. Smultea, courtesy of Pacific Whale Foundation

# How much do calves weigh when they are born?

The birth weight of calves depends on the species. A Fin Whale calf will weigh 3,600 pounds (1,630kg) at birth, while a Humpback calf will weigh 1,800 pounds (810kg).

▶ **Calves of baleen whales, such as a Blue Whale calf, may weigh as much as 4,400 pounds (1,995 kg).**

By Thomas Jefferson

# How long are calves when they are born?

Again, size depends on the species. Blue Whale calves measure 25 feet (6–7m) long when they are born. The Humpback Whale is 14 feet (4.2m) long at birth.

By Thomas Jefferson

◀ **This Humpback calf may make noises to communicate with its mother, but, like other whales, it does not cry.**

## How does a calf eat?

The calf holds onto one of the mother's nipples as the mother squirts milk into the calf's mouth. This is different from most land mammals, who suck on the mother's nipple.

## How often does a calf eat?

A calf may nurse from its mother as often as 40 times a day! The feeding times are very short, since the calf must continually surface for air.

## How long are baby whales called calves?

For the first few months of their lives. Then, as the calves grow up, they are called "juveniles."

By Mari A. Smultea, courtesy of Pacific Whale Foundation

▲ **The mother's nipples are hidden in the mammary slits on each side of the genital slit on the underside of the whale, as with this Humpback Whale.**

► Calves look a lot like their parents when they are born, like this Right Whale calf.

By Dr. Bernd Würsig

## Do whales make good parents?

Males travel to different nursery schools to breed, and they do not stay with the females. Therefore, they never bond with their offspring. Females and calves, though, form a very strong bond.

▼ Whales are often studied from airplanes. This mother and baby Southern Right Whale were photographed from a plane.

By Mari A. Smultea, courtesy of Pacific Whale Foundation

Dr. Bernd Würsig

▲ Female whales are excellent parents, and the mother guards and protects her offspring for (depending on the species) the first 24 months of life.

54

## How long do calves stay with their mothers?

In most toothed whale species, the pod, made up of females and their offspring, stays together throughout the animals' lives. The female calves never really leave their mothers or the other caregivers in the nursery school. They just gradually start feeding on their own. The males leave the pod in order to mate with females of other pods. Some of them come back, and some of them form temporary pods of their own. Male and female baleen whale calves separate from their mothers after a year or two and never really form permanent pods.

By D. Rugh

▲ **This mother Bowhead Whale is keeping a close eye on her calf and will fight off any possible predator.**

## How soon can a mother whale have a second calf?

Whales usually have a calf only every two or three years. By that time, the first calf has grown up and is taking care of itself. If a mother has twins—which is very rare—one usually dies, because it is difficult to tend to two calves.

## How soon is a whale ready to have babies?

Depending upon the species, whales are 11 years old or more before they mate and have calves of their own.

# SELF-DEFENSE

*Life as a whale can be hard. Predators are always lurking, waiting for the opportunity to feed. Male whales must compete for mates. Whales are at the mercy of humans, who hunt them and poison their environment. Whales have no defense against humans. It is up to us to protect them and their environment.*

◀ **Humpback Whales can slap their tails in the water so loudly it sounds like a rifle shot.**

By Gene Kent

▲ **This Humpback Whale may be warning competitors that it is big and powerful. The crashing sound as it hits the water can be heard for miles.**

## Who are a whale's enemies?

Orcas, or Killer Whales, polar bears, and sharks are among the whale's natural enemies. However, humans are the most dangerous enemies of whales.

**57**

## How have humans hurt whales?

With whale hunting, humans have greatly reduced the whale population. Some species are almost extinct. Pollution is also responsible for the death of many whales. Poisonous chemicals build up in the whale's body, causing cancer and many other fatal diseases.

▼ **Thousands of whales are accidentally or deliberately injured or killed each year by humans. This Humpback Whale is missing half of its tail fin. It may have been struck by a ship.**

By Richard A. Rowlett, IUIB

By Mari A. Smultea, courtesy of Pacific Whale Foundation

▲ **Orcas hunt in packs, attacking and eating even the largest whales. Here, a Minke Whale is being chased by a pair of Orcas. The Orcas swim ahead of the whale and below it, to prevent it from diving. They take bites out of it until it gets tired.**

By Mari A. Smultea, courtesy of Pacific Whale Foundation

◀ The injury to the dorsal fin and back of this Humpback Whale was probably caused by a ship's propeller.

▼ When a whale is sick or hurt, other whales swim close to it and even push it to the surface to breathe. When it gets well, the animal will help others of its pod in the same way.

## How do whales protect themselves?

Whales use their powerful tails to fight enemies, or dive to avoid them. When a whale is injured or sick, other whales gather around the weakened whale to protect it.

By Mari A. Smultea, courtesy of Pacific Whale Foundation

# Do whales fight among themselves?

Yes, males not only fight each other for mating rights, but also for the best feeding opportunities. Another kind of whale, the Narwhal, uses its tusks like a sword when battling other Narwhals. Many species have scars on their bodies from battling.

By Mari A. Smultea, courtesy of Pacific Whale Foundation

◀ Humpback Whales warn other whales of their presence by slapping the water with their fins.

▼ When Humpbacks fight, they can be seen "head lunging." It's called "head lunging" when the whales speed towards each other with their heads out of the water.

By Mari A. Smultea, courtesy of Pacific Whale Foundation

By Mari A. Smultea, courtesy of Pacific Whale Foundation

◄ These two Humpback Whales are fighting in a way that's called "head butting." It can cause scraping and even bleeding, but it doesn't injure the whales seriously.

▼ Dolphins often threaten each other by shaking their bodies or clapping their jaws. They will ram each other and sometimes even bite. These Spinner Dolphins are fighting.

By Richard A. Rowlett, IUIB

▲ The white scrapes on this Southern Bottlenose Whale are tooth marks from fighting with other members of its species. Rarely seen, this whale was photographed just southwest of Australia in the Indian Ocean.

By Gene Kent

# WHALES AND PEOPLE

*In some countries around the world, the whale is worshipped and loved. Other countries destroy this beautiful animal for food, products, or just for "sport." This destruction has caused massive decreases in the numbers of whales over the years.*

◄ **In 1991, these three whales were found trapped by ice, unable to reach the open sea. Many countries cooperated in saving them.**

## Are whales friendly to people?

Whales seem to be interested in people. There are reports of whales swimming close to boats as if they thought the vessel was another animal. However, they seem to know that the boats have people on them.

▼ **Like other whales, Grey Whales seem to be curious about people and to enjoy being touched by them. But no one can be sure what the whales are feeling.**

By Thomas Jefferson

By Michael Philo

**63**

## Are whales afraid of humans?

If not, they should be. Whale hunters have taken advantage of the whales' gentle nature and peaceful curiosity. They have devised many techniques for trapping and killing whales. One of them has been to capture the calf to draw in the mother, and then kill the mother as she tries to defend it.

## How long have people hunted whales?

While native people have hunted whales for many thousands of years, whaling didn't become a big industry until the 1600s, when Dutch, English and American whaling ships began sailing the seas. Japan started catching whales with huge nets in the mid-1600s. Then Norway introduced the exploding harpoon gun and the steam-powered whaling ship in the 1800s, which was the start of modern whaling, the most destructive type. Large numbers of whales were killed.

By Mari A. Smultea, courtesy of Pacific Whale Foundation

◄ Eskimos have hunted whales for hundreds of years, but they catch only enough for survival. They kill the whales for their oil, blubber and meat. The Eskimos have never endangered any whale species.

▼ Humpback Whales show little fear of humans. They come so close to boats they sometimes bump into them.

By Kathleen Dudzinski

**64**

# How are whales hunted now?

Whalers use radar and even helicopters to spot whales. They harpoon the animals and then tag them with a radio transmitter. Another ship, as large as an aircraft carrier, comes along and picks up the dead whale.

Meanwhile, the first ship hunts for the next whale. International regulations have put a stop to much of the killing, but not all countries observe the laws. Norway and Japan kill hundreds of whales each year.

By Richard A. Rowlett, IUIB

▲ The Right Whale got its name from being "the right whale to kill." It was slow and easy to catch; it floated after it died; and it provided huge amounts of blubber and oil.

# What are gill or drift nets?

They are huge nets used by fishermen to catch large numbers of fish and squid. Often dolphins, whales, birds, turtles, seals, sea lions, and sharks blunder into these nets accidentally and die.

▼ This whaling station is still operating today.

By Jon Stern

## What products are made from whales?

Whale meat had been used as food by Eskimos, Native Americans, and the Japanese before European whaling started. Whale oil was once used for making candles, soap, and crayons. Spermaceti (see page 26) was used in cosmetics and skin cleansers. Blubber was boiled down into oil for lamps and for lubricating machinery. Teeth and bones were used in jewelry. Tendons became strings for tennis rackets and thread for surgery. Whale bones were made into fishing poles and frames for houses.

**▲ This was once a Humpback Whale. Its skin has been used to make shoelaces and saddles. The skeletal remains have been used as fertilizer, as glue, and in food products. Its skull is all that is left.**

## What should I do if I see a stranded whale?

Get help from a policeman, a lifeguard, the local stranding network, or the Coast Guard. If the animal is alive, keep its blowhole clear. Try to keep the animal damp and cool by patting it with wet towels or seaweed.

## Is it dangerous to touch it?

It's dangerous for the whale. A stranded whale should be kept as calm as possible. Its skin is sensitive and fragile when the animal is out of the water.

**► Years ago, many people thought stranded whales, such as this Grey Whale, were terrible monsters from the sea.**

By Thomas Jefferson

◀ **This Pygmy Sperm Whale was found along the beach. It is one of many species that strand themselves, perhaps by losing their way in the open sea.**

## Where can I go to see whales?

Today many people "whale watch" all over the world. Several travel companies have special tours that include whale watching. Many natural history museums display whale bones and models.

▶ **Whale watching is an excellent opportunity to view whales close up. The best time to see these Grey Whales is during their winter and summer migrations.**

By Thomas Jefferson

# If I studied whales, what could I be?

Marine biologists specialize in the study of whales, dolphins, and porpoises.

▶ **This research boat, named the Oregon Two, is used by marine biologists to study whales.**

▼ **Its specialized computers process information on such things as migration, population, and feeding.**

By NOAA: Wayne Hoggard

By NOAA: Wayne Hoggard

◀ Scientists use special binoculars to see whales that surface from far away.

## Do many governments study whales?

Yes, many countries, in cooperation with the International Whaling Commission, study whale population, migration, and the effects of humans on whales.

▶ This Twin Otter airplane is used by the U.S. Government to find whales quickly from the air.

## Are all whales protected?

In 1985, the International Whaling Commission banned all commercial whaling, but some countries still hunt whales. Japan and Norway claim that they hunt them for scientific research, but whale meat is sold in stores and restaurants in those countries.

▶ **In all U.S. waters, whales, such as this Grey Whale, are protected by the Marine Mammal Act of 1972. This act prevents people from swimming with marine mammals, feeding them, or approaching them in boats and planes.**

## What can I do to protect whales?

There are many different organizations you can join to help protect and conserve the whales of the world. Ask your local librarian for information on organizations in your area.

▲ **Many major university programs, such as the Marine Mammal Research Program at Texas A & M University in Galveston, Texas, specialize in studying marine mammals and human impact on them.**

## What is Greenpeace?

This environmental organization tries to help endangered animals. The Greenpeace people go out to sea and position their boat between the whale and the whaling ship to try to prevent the ship from firing at the whale. These actions have gotten worldwide attention, which Greenpeace hopes will pressure all whaling operations to stop.

▲ **Although commercial whaling was banned in 1985, the I.W.C. still allows Alaskan Eskimos to hunt whales to support their families.**

## What is the Worldwide Fund for Nature?

This organization, which raises money for conservation, has greatly helped whale conservation projects worldwide.

## What is CITES?

CITES (the Convention on International Trade in Endangered Species) was created in the 1960s to protect species that are threatened by international trade. CITES would protect whales if all countries observed the regulations.

# GREAT WHALES

## How many kinds of whales are there?

The 13 families of whales are each a little different from the others. In those families are 77 different species—or kinds—of whales, dolphins, and porpoises. For example:

A **family** of whales is the Rorqual Whales.
A **species** of Rorqual Whale is the Blue Whale.

A **family** of whales is the Right Whales.
A **species** of Right Whale is the Bowhead Whale.

▶ **The Blue Whale has been hunted to the point of near-extinction. Although the animal is now protected, it is not yet certain that the species will survive.**

## What is a Rorqual Whale family like?

Rorquals are baleen whales that have grooves or pleats in their throats (see page 41). There are six species: the Blue Whale, the Fin Whale, the Sei Whale, the Bryde's Whale, the Minke Whale, and the Humpback Whale.

## The Blue Whale

The Blue Whale is the largest animal on earth. It once grew as long as 100 feet (30.5m) and weighed up to 150 tons (136,000kg), but today it is smaller. Females are bigger than males. Blue Whales are usually loners. Small numbers of them are found in open oceans all over the world.

By Dr. Bernd Würsig

## The Fin Whale

Nicknamed "razorback" for its sharp dorsal fin, Fin Whales are the second-largest of all the whales. Their slender bodies are designed for great speed. They are usually 65 to 70 feet (20–21m) long and weigh up to 60 tons (54,000kg). Fin Whales are found in oceans all over the world.

By Dr. Bernd Würsig

▲ **The Fin Whale's great speed—it can swim up to 25 miles (40km) per hour—helps it escape predators, such as the Killer Whale.**

## The Minke Whale

The smallest whale of the Rorqual family, the Minke Whale grows from 26 to 30 feet (8 to 9m) long, and weighs around 10 tons (9,000kg). Minke Whales live in all the world's oceans.

▶ **The Minke Whale is nicknamed "little piked" and "little finner." Fisheries in Japan and Korea have killed a lot of Minke Whales.**

By Thomas Jefferson

# The Humpback Whale

One of this whale's most remarkable features is its wing-like flippers, which are longer than the flippers of any other whale. The flippers alone may be as long as 14 feet (4.2m)!

Humpback Whales grow up to 60 feet (18m) long and weigh as much as 40 tons (36,000kg). They live in oceans all over the world.

▼ **This whale may have gotten its name for the way it breaches. It leaps completely out of the water and then dives back into the water in a bent or "humpbacked" position.**

By Gene Kent

## What is the Grey Whale family like?

This family has only one species, the Grey Whale.

## The Grey Whale

Grey Whales measure between 40 and 50 feet (12.2 and 15.2m) and weigh as much as 73,000 pounds (33,000kg). Instead of a dorsal fin, this whale has little "humps" along the lower half of its back. Grey Whales swim close to the shore in the North Pacific Ocean around Canada, Alaska, and California.

## What is the Right Whale family like?

Fatter and rounder than other whales, Right Whales are the slowest swimmers. They have no dorsal fin. There are three species: the Southern Right Whale, the Northern Right Whale, and the Bowhead Whale.

By D.E. Withrow

▲ The Grey Whale is the most primitive whale. It looks more like ancient whales than any other whale living today.

## What is the Pygmy Right Whale family like?

This family has only one species—the Pygmy Right Whale. It is rarely seen, but studies have been done on strandings found in Australia, New Zealand, and South Africa.

## The Bowhead Whale

The Bowhead Whale, named for the extreme curve of its huge lower jaw, is also called the Greenland Right Whale. Very stocky, with an enormous head that is almost one-third the size of its body, the Bowhead can grow up to 65 feet (20m) and weigh 122 tons (110,678kg). The Bowhead lives in cold Arctic waters, where it uses its size and strength to break holes in the ice for breathing.

## What is the Sperm Whale family like?

This family has a squarish head with only one blowhole. It has three species: the Sperm Whale, the Pygmy Sperm Whale, and the Dwarf Sperm Whale.

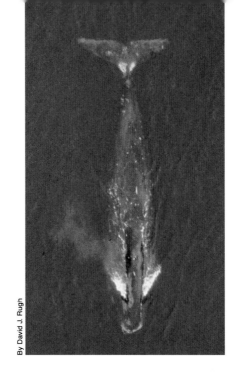

By David J. Rugh

◄ **Once killed in great numbers by whalers, the Bowhead is endangered. There is great concern about whether conservation efforts will be able to save it.**

▼ **Moby Dick, in the famous book by Herman Melville, was a Sperm Whale.**

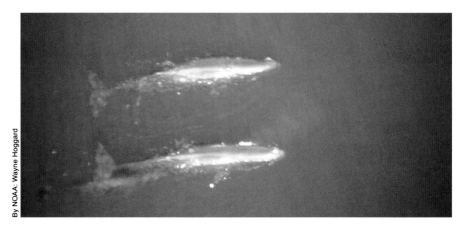

By NOAA: Wayne Hoggard

## The Sperm Whale

The largest toothed whale, the Sperm Whale grows to about 60 feet (18.5m) in length. Instead of a dorsal fin, it has a ridge of bumps on its back.

The whale is rusty black or dark grey with deep creases or wrinkles all over its body. It is found throughout the world except in ice-packed waters.

## What is the White Whale family like?

Two species make up the White Whale family—the Beluga Whale and the Narwhal Whale. Both have swollen foreheads and flexible necks so they can turn their heads. Other than that, the Beluga and Narwhal don't look alike.

## The Beluga

The Beluga is dark brown or blue-grey when it is born, but as it gets older, the colors fade until it is totally white. It may grow as long as 16 feet (5m) and weigh up to 2,400 pounds (1,100kg).

## The Narwhal

The Narwhal Whale got its name from an ancient Scandinavian word that describes its streaky, spotted skin. The male Narwhal has a long tusk that is actually an overgrown tooth; it grows forward from the whale's mouth. The tusk is 8 to 9 feet (2.5 to 2.8m) long. The Narwhal lives in the icy waters of the North Polar region.

**▼ The highly endangered Narwhal is one of the most unusual-looking whales. It is still hunted by poachers for its tusk, often compared to the horn of the mythical unicorn.**

By Jeffrey L. Martin

By Richard A. Rowlett, IUIB

**◄ Because it chirps when it is at the surface, the Beluga has been nicknamed "sea canary."**

By Michael Newcomer

## What is the Beaked Whale family like?

These medium-sized, toothed whales are rare, or at least seldom seen. They got their name from their snout, which looks like a bird's beak. They have a small dorsal fin and fairly small flippers. There are ten species.

## Baird's Beaked Whale

The largest of the Beaked Whales, the Baird's Beaked Whale grows up to 40 feet (12m) long and weighs as much as 12 tons (10,886kg). It lives in the North Pacific Ocean from Japan to California to the Bering Sea (between Alaska and Siberia).

▲ The Baird's Beaked Whale is nicknamed "the giant bottlenose whale" because of its huge beak, which is more than 6½ feet (2m) long.

By Mari A. Smultea, courtesy of Pacific Whale Foundation

## What other families of whales are there?

Other families include dolphins and porpoises.

## Orca, or Killer Whale

The Killer Whale, or Orca, is a dolphin. It has striking black and white coloring. An adult male can grow more than 31 feet (9.5m) in length and weigh over eight tons (7,200kg). Females are much smaller than males.

## Dall's Porpoise

Named after the American zoologist, William Healey Dall, who discovered it, this porpoise lives in the North Pacific. It grows to seven feet (2.1m) and weighs as much as 480 pounds (218kg). It is the fastest and strongest of all whales.

▲ False Killer Whales, like Killer Whales, have a large dorsal fin, so they are sometimes mistaken for them. However, they are much smaller—20 feet (6m) and 3,000 pounds (1350kg). They also lack the bold white markings of the Orca.

▼ The plump, muscled body of the Dall's Porpoise is built to go fast. It reaches full speed almost instantly.

By Thomas Jefferson

# Acknowledgments

We have many scientists and photographers to thank for their help with our book. It is no exaggeration to say that this project would have been impossible without them. Their devotion to their calling has resulted in a storehouse of high-quality information and materials. They have selflessly shared this wealth with us, and we owe them everything. We cannot possibly do them justice in the space allowed, but we will give it our best.

Texas A&M University Marine Mammal Research Program in Galveston. Dr. Bernd Würsig, Dr. Graham Worthy, Thomas Jefferson, Barbara Curry, Jon Stern, Bill Stevens, Terry Christopher, and Dagmar Fertl.
Kathleen Dudzinski, Oceanic Society Expeditions.
Mari A. Smultea, Pacific Whale Foundation.

Tom La Puzza, Public Affairs Officer, United States Navy.
The Texas Marine Mammal Stranding Network.
Dr. Jim Hain, Associated Scientists at Woods Hole.
David Withrow, Robin Angliss, David Rugh, Dr. Howard Braham, and Sally Mizroch, of the National Marine Mammal Laboratory in Seattle.
Michael Philo, North Slope Borough, Barrow, Alaska.
Dr. Wayne Vogl and David Pfeiffer at the University of British Columbia.
Rocky Strong, Gene Kent, Michael W. Newcomer, and the Steinhart Aquarium at the California Academy of Sciences.
Richard A. Rowlett, International Union of Itinerate Biologists.
Southeast Fisheries Center, Mississippi Laboratories, NOAA: Wayne Hoggard, Lesley V. Higgins, Carol L. Roden, Ian Workman, and Keith D. Mullen.

# Index

10